OUT OF THE DEPTHS

THE BLUE WHALE STORY

MARK ENGSTROM · BURTON LIM · JACQUELINE MILLER

OLIVER HADDRATH · DAVE IRELAND · GERRY DE IULIIS

ROYAL ONTARIO MUSEUM

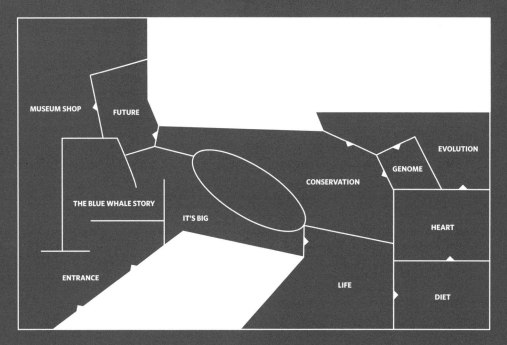

MUSEUM SHOP

FUTURE

EVOLUTION

THE BLUE WHALE STORY

CONSERVATION

GENOME

IT'S BIG

HEART

ENTRANCE

LIFE

DIET

Exhibit Floor Plan

CONTENTS

Measuring the
24-m long Trout
River blue whale.

FOREWORD

The quest for discovery through research is a testament to the ROM's commitment to expanding our collective knowledge. Our scientists and researchers are passionate about highlighting important issues across the globe that might otherwise be overlooked. In doing so, we illuminate the many connections between humanity and the world around us.

The story of the ROM salvaging two blue whales, that washed upon the shores of Newfoundland in 2014, exemplifies how our curatorial research helps us better understand the world. The ROM's expedition to Newfoundland has resulted in the *Out of the Depths: The Blue Whale Story* exhibition, featuring the spectacle of the largest creature that ever lived. This guide to the exhibition is not only a companion to the arresting display at the ROM, but also a deeper dive into the still-mysterious world of blue whale biology and evolution. It uncovers fascinating new scientific insights into these resilient creatures. This publication not only deepens our knowledge of the whale's surprising biology and under-sea life, but also proposes how we can help save the blue whale from extinction. If we succeed, we will save the marine ecosystems upon which the blue whale, and humanity, depend on.

I would like to thank the creators of the exhibition, Dr. Mark Engstrom and Dr. Burton Lim, Jacqueline Miller, Oliver Haddrath, Dave Ireland, and Dr. Gerry De Iuliis, for writing this enlightening publication while simultaneously developing the exhibition.

Several generous donors and sponsors have invested in this project. I would like to thank the Louise Hawley Stone Charitable Trust for funding this publication and providing financial support for the Blue Whale Project. Special thanks also goes to our donors and patrons, EQ Bank, J. Crew, Alan and Patricia Koval Foundation, Jean M. Read, and Nita and Donald Reed, who generously supported the Blue Whale Project.

Josh Basseches
Director & CEO

In this Medieval bestiary, the whale is so big that sailors mistake it for an island and land on its back. When the whale awakens, legend portends that the men will be dragged to the ocean depths by the great malevolent beast.

INTRODUCTION

Blue whales have captured our collective imagination and awed us for thousands of years. Before we learned of their remarkable evolutionary history, or found fossil evidence of ancestral whales, or even before we knew that they were, in fact, mammals, blue whales spawned images and stories of sea monsters—devilish, living islands that trapped unwitting sailors—and mysterious ocean life. By the 1970s, the image of blue whales was transformed as the positive focus of an environmental movement to protect our oceans and nature in general.

To this day, so much of the natural history of blue whales remains a mystery: we don't know where they go to breed, we don't know how their global populations are connected, and we don't know the secrets that lie within their genetic code. Unlocking these mysteries may shed light on these great leviathans and help us better understand the delicate ecology of our oceans.

The unfortunate death of nine blue whales in 2014 and the ROM's salvage of two that washed ashore in Newfoundland presented us with an opportunity to help demystify the blue whale. As you will learn in this book, the ROM is decoding the entire genome of the blue whale for the first time, and our anatomical work on the skeletons and heart from the recovered specimens is bringing into focus the picture of their extreme adaptations.

Blue whales, and whales in general, are excellent flagship species for the conservation of our ocean environments. They inhabit so many different ocean ecosystems that protecting them will benefit countless other species, and their place in our imagination connects us to their plight.

The ROM has an unprecedented chance to contribute to a better global understanding of the biology and preservation of the largest animal to have ever lived on Earth. We hope that you will join us in this awe-inspiring story of discovery as it unfolds in this exhibition and at the Museum over the next several years.

THE ROM STORY

In March 2014, several whales were sighted trapped in ice formations in the Gulf of St. Lawrence. This report triggered a sequence of events and discoveries that continue to this day.

DEAD WHALES IN THE GULF

The whales spotted in 2014 were about 100 kilometres from the southwestern tip of the island of Newfoundland, near the Cabot Strait between Newfoundland and Nova Scotia. Dr. Jack Lawson, a researcher with the federal Department of Fisheries and Oceans (DFO) in St. John's, flew over the area and verified that nine blue whales were dead in the ice floes. Several others were spotted to the southeast, alive and swimming.

Nobody knows exactly when or how these blue whales died, but their death is significant. The International Union for the Conservation of Nature classifies the blue whale as a globally endangered species; it is also protected under Canadian law by the Species at Risk Act. Although a ban on hunting blue whales has been in effect for more than 50 years, their numbers remain dangerously low with an estimated 20,000 individuals worldwide. The northwestern Atlantic population is the smallest, at only 200–400 whales, so the death of nine adult whales threatens its continued existence.

THE LIKELY CAUSE OF DEATH

Blue whales feed exclusively on tiny crustaceans called krill. As temperatures rise in late winter and early spring, huge swarms of krill emerge in the Gulf of St. Lawrence, which blue whales track in search of food. The winter of 2014 was unusually cold and the build-up of ice in the Gulf was heavy. Blue whales in the area were likely already feeding when ice shifted just north of where two currents pass through the Cabot Strait. The nine blues spotted in March may have become trapped in or under the ice. There was damage to the skulls of the two whales that eventually beached and were salvaged on the west coast of Newfoundland, suggesting that the ice had crushed them. We are not sure, however, if it happened before or after death.

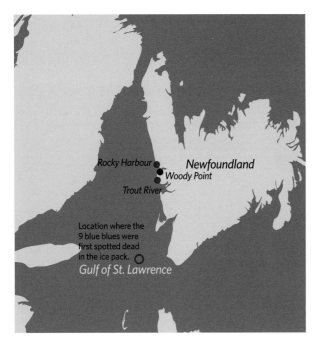

Map of Newfoundland where two blue whales washed ashore in 2014 at Trout River and Rocky Harbour. The Trout River whale was towed to Woody Point where it was processed.

THE ROM STEPS UP

by Mark Engstrom

For a decade before these blue whale deaths, the ROM had been slowly and opportunistically accumulating a collection of whales that had washed ashore on the east and west coasts of Canada. Specimens of fin, minke, humpback, killer, right, and sperm whales had already been salvaged and cleaned. The ultimate goal is a permanent gallery at the ROM of all species of large whales that are found in Canadian waters.

When Lois Harwood of the DFO alerted me to the tragic discovery in Newfoundland, I immediately contacted Dr. Lawson and asked him to let me know if, by chance, one of the blues drifted ashore—a rare occurrence because most dead blue whales sink. A month later, against all odds, residents in Trout River and Rocky Harbour, Newfoundland, saw floating masses on the horizon that eventually washed ashore—two blue whales.

The beached whales caused a world-wide sensation, but behind the scenes and away from the hubbub, the DFO and the ROM were in discussions to recover the whales for scientific research and educational purposes. In short order, we reached an agreement which was formally announced on the floor of the House of Commons on May 1, 2014, by the Minister of Fisheries and Oceans. And then the paperwork and logistics began!

Bloated blue whale that washed ashore at Trout River in late April 2014.

ALL IN A WEEK'S WORK

Salvaging two magnificent examples of the largest animal that has ever lived required a team of resourceful people possessing a wide range of skill sets—from biologists to heavy equipment operators, politicians and government staffers. My role in the project was to be decisive, trust my partners, have an unwavering vision, and to cross my fingers and believe, even when the reality of financial backing was at times dubious. I wore a number of hats during the two weeks in Newfoundland that followed my initial e-mail contact with Dr. Lawson. I was simultaneously the media spokesperson for the ROM and the liaison between the federal and provincial agencies. On top of that, I was fundraising, hiring local contractor Don Allen in Newfoundland to help salvage the whales, and obtaining permits for opening new landfills, and bringing in a crew from Research Casting International to help process and ship the whale to their facility in Trenton, Ontario. A typical day while flensing a 90-tonne whale also involved giving multiple media interviews. At the same time, I was able to negotiate an agreement with Memorial University to cover the costs of processing and mounting one of the whales to be displayed on the University's St. John's campus.

Had I known what we were getting into, would I do it again? You bet. This has been one of the most rewarding projects I have ever been involved with. Great rewards follow significant efforts (and equal bits of bullheadedness and faith)—as one newspaper article so prophetically headlined, "No Guts, No Glory!"

The recovery team at Woody Point in front of the Trout River blue whale skull: Sean Barnes, Eddie Samms, Robert Gammon, Brett Crawford, Mike Thom, Aaron Thom, Burton Lim, Mark Engstrom, and Richard Roberts.

RECOVERING THE BEACHED WHALES

by Burton Lim

We arrived in Newfoundland in early May...to snowfall. And this was just our first challenge. The Trout River whale was half submerged in the bay along a boulder-strewn shoreline below a boardwalk—an untenable situation. The best alternative was to work in Woody Point, 20 kilometres away by road. During a specially-called meeting and a close vote (3–2!), Woody Point's town council gave us approval and the whale was towed by trawler on a two-hour journey through the open sea to the fish processing plant in town.

Another challenge: how to get rid of the tons of blubber, flesh, and guts that could not be discarded into the water because of public health concerns? The municipality authorized a special dump site that was lined with crushed limestone to neutralize contaminants leaching into the soil from decomposition.

The salvage team was a diverse crew. Mark Engstrom and I represented the ROM and were joined by Brett Crawford, Mike Thom, Aaron Thom, and Peter Root of Research Casting International (RCI)—specialists in preparing large-animal displays for museums and experienced whale disassemblers. We also needed the help of four local folks—Eddie Samms, Sean Barnes, Robert Gammon, and Richard Roberts—with tough constitutions, strong stomachs, and resourcefulness. (A poor sense of smell was also an asset!)

The dirty, smelly, back-breaking work of reducing a 24-metre, 90-tonne beast to a pile of bones began. It took the 10 of us working 6 days for 12 hours each day to complete the job. Luckily, we had access to heavy equipment on-site including a front-end loader, forklift, and dump truck—otherwise it would have taken twice as long! This memorable experience was made even better by the hospitality shown to us on the Rock. We were warmly welcomed into homes, lodgings, restaurants, and shops—and only occasionally did anyone point out (with a smile) that we reeked like dead whales.

Two weeks after we left, ROM Mammalogy Technician Jacqueline Miller returned with a slightly reconstituted team to process the Rocky Harbour blue whale, this time salvaging not only the bones but also the heart.

Beginning to flense in sections the skin and blubber of the tail from the Trout River blue whale at Woody Point.

CLEANING THE BONES FOR DISPLAY

Two eighteen-wheelers were needed to transport the whale bones and heart to RCI's headquarters in Trenton, Ontario—one for the two skulls and one for the remaining parts. In Trenton, holes were cut into the tops of our now-useless trailer containers (once you transport a dead whale in a container, the lingering smell ensures nobody will want to use it again) and steaming manure from a large number of cows was added to bury the bones—for two years. This was especially needed for the skull, flippers, and tail, which had been difficult to skin to the bone. Fresh local manure was ordered and delivered to RCI in six dump trucks. Manure and bones were layered in the empty shipping containers, with weeping tile inserted to allow air to circulate and supply the microbes with oxygen to speed the composting. The skulls needed frequent monitoring because they were partially damaged in the ice, and so were only superficially defleshed in order to protect the fragile bones during transport from Newfoundland.

Two other blue whales on display in Canada used different methods for the initial cleaning. The Canadian Museum of Nature buried their defleshed whale in the ground for eight years before degreasing the bones. The whole body of the blue whale at the University of British Columbia's Beaty Museum was buried in sand on a beach for over 20 years and the bones still needed to be defleshed.

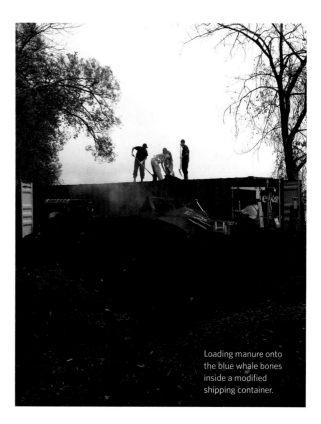

Loading manure onto the blue whale bones inside a modified shipping container.

Blue whale bones after composting in manure and awaiting degreasing at RCI.

A detergent spray degreasing the natural oils in the bones of the blue whale.

After removing the bones from the compost in June 2016, the next major task was to remove the oil from the bones. Visitors to the blue whale exhibition would not be pleased with rancid whale oil dripping on them. With most other animals, the whole skeleton can be put into a large vat of water or detergent to leach out the fat in the bones. But the blue whale has huge bones—some of its ribs are over 2 metres long! And forget about finding a container for its skull. Never backing down from a challenge, RCI built a "car wash" fit for a blue whale. Our whales didn't move through the wash the way a car would; instead, a mild solution of detergent constantly sprayed the bones to dissolve out the greasy contents—all done in an above-ground swimming pool.

Once degreased, the bones were ready to be mounted for display as an articulated skeleton. A large steel rod was custom made to support the underside of the skeleton and attached to supporting plates placed between the vertebrae holding each element in place without damaging the bone. Each bone can be easily removed for study as needed. These bones are important specimens, not simply props. The complete skeleton consists of five main sections: skull, chest and trunk, tail, and two flippers. Two trucks were required to deliver the skeleton for final assembly in the exhibition hall by RCI. Our blue whale is positioned in a racing pose ("coursing") and fills the full height of the 5-metre-high exhibition room. Visitors can walk around the complete skeleton, even under its tail.

The beginning of the re-articulation process for displaying the Trout River blue whale skeleton. From right to left, the cervical (neck) and thoracic (chest) vertebrae being mounted on the supporting armature.

PRESERVING A WHALE OF A HEART

by Jacqueline Miller

It is a rare and valuable opportunity to salvage two blue whale skeletons. It is rarer still to be able to salvage the intact heart of a blue whale. The Rocky Harbour whale provided that opportunity. For the first time ever, a complete blue whale heart will be available for public viewing and scientific study.

How did this come about? At Trout River, Mark Engstrom, the force behind the blue whale project, lamented that people always asked him how big a blue whale heart was. He thought if only we had one, we could just point and say, "That's how big." What an idea! Could we recover the heart from the Rocky Harbour whale? About this time, Dr. Paul Nader, a large-animal veterinarian from Lincoln Memorial University, Tennessee, contacted Mark. He had heard about our project and enthusiastically volunteered for the Rocky Harbour salvage. He was especially keen to advise on recovering the heart. Dr. Nader said the best way to preserve the heart for science was to plastinate it—and it just so happened that not only did Dr. Nader know how to plastinate, but at LMU he worked with one of the world's leading authorities on the subject, Dr. Robert Henry.

EXTRACTING THE ROCKY HARBOUR BLUE WHALE HEART

PLUGGING UP BLOOD VESSELS

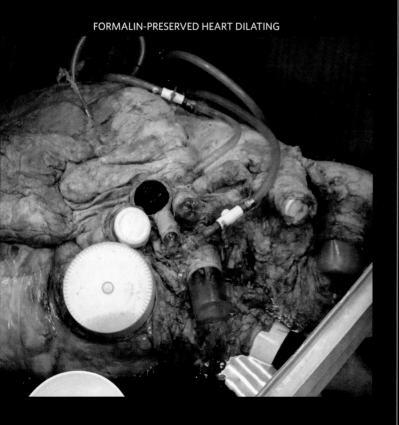

FORMALIN-PRESERVED HEART DILATING

WHAT IS PLASTINATION?

Plastination is a process for preserving bodies or body parts by replacing all of the water in their cells with long-lasting polymers like silicone. The complete process takes time because it involves several iterative processes. First, you exchange all the water in the cells with acetone, a process called dehydration. Then place the dehydrated, acetone saturated specimen in a polymer bath of silicone. Everything is then placed in a vacuum chamber where pressure is gradually dropped to almost zero—close to the condition in outer space! This drop in pressure causes the acetone to bubble away, while the vacuum forces the silicone into the space where the acetone was in the cells. When this final stage of silicone impregnation is complete with the last of the acetone gone, the heart is hardened, or cured. In the end, our plastinated heart will retain fine anatomical details for hundreds of years.

Dr. Vladimir Chereminskiy from Gubener Plastinate dissecting the epicardium to create a viewing window of the inside of the heart. Cardiac blood vessels are also exposed.

Unable to remain for the entire whale salvage in May 2014, Dr. Nader advised me on how to extract the heart if it appeared to be in good condition. Well, it was—and what a job extraction proved to be! Immense and unwieldy, the heart had to be severed at its great vessels and carefully pushed into a huge dumpster bag to be lifted away. We froze the heart and stored it at RCI until Drs. Nader and Henry were able to join us for the next step: dilating the heart and preserving it in formaldehyde.

It was daunting work. Understanding anatomy from a text book or from smaller specimens is not the same as trying to orient oneself to an actual blue whale heart spread out over a dissection table or floating in a hot tub–sized tank. We were successful, but we had to do considerable preparatory work over several months while we decided on the next steps for our blue whale heart and the hearts from several other species that were being plastinated for comparison. Each had its challenges. Plastination requires creating a vacuum to impregnate the heart with polymer, and for a specimen as large as our blue's heart, we needed a chamber as strong as a submarine or space ship! We don't have anything like this in Canada... but Germany does. The Von Hagen family company, Gubener Plastinate GmbH, took over the job, while the rest of us monitored the "pulse" of the operation.

MEDIA MADNESS

The blue whale has received the most media coverage by far of any project in the history of the ROM. Interest has been intense in Canada and around the world. During our two-week stay in Newfoundland to recover the Trout River whale, not a day went by without stories appearing on the front page of newspapers, on televised nightly news, or in blog posts.

Interest started locally, with Newfoundland's NTV, spread nationally to *The National Post* and *The Globe and Mail*, and then internationally to the BBC and Al Jazeera—to name just a few. A *Toronto Star* reporter was on-site at Woody Point all week to document our daily progress. Social media buzzed with retweets and likes on Twitter and Facebook. Several media outlets, such as the Discovery Channel's *Daily Planet*, have reported on every stage of the project, from the salvaging of the Trout River whale to the burying of bones in manure and the plastination of the heart of the Rocky Harbour whale. Blue whale articles have also been published by *The New Yorker*, *The Walrus*, and *The Wall Street Journal*.

Even *Saturday Night Live* took notice. On the weekend we were skinning the Trout River whale, the comedy show included a skit called "Bikini Beach Party" in which actors Taran Killam and Charlize Theron (playing a parody of Gidget) were sprayed with blood and guts from not one but two exploding blue whales! It was the crescendo of our 15 minutes of fame—and we missed it because we had another earlier morning meeting with a real whale.

WHY SHOULD WE CARE

All life on Earth—or biodiversity—is incredibly interconnected. All organisms are important for maintaining our environment: our clean water, fresh air, and the food we all eat. Blue whales are important for maintaining our ecosystems because they are part of this fabric of life.

Iconic, mysterious, and charismatic species, like the blue whale, offer unique opportunities for inspiring the public. Preserving the world's megafauna will go a long way to preserving other life. During the 1970s, the blue whale was used as a symbol for environmental campaigns encouraging ocean and whale conservation.

Blue whales hold incredible research value and can help us understand how life evolved, and how mammals adapted to life in the oceans. Much of their biology remains a mystery, and our understanding of their ecology (how and where they eat, mate, and move) is still poorly understood. We do know that they are adapted to life in all oceans except the high Arctic, so protecting blue whale habitat protects a lot of ocean!

Whales are ecosystem engineers and are very important in marine food webs in two big ways. A dead whale will usually sink, and this nutrient and carbon boost to the ocean floor is an ecosystem in and of itself. During life, whales produce a lot of poop—the feces contain crucially important nutrients for the base of the very food web that sustains them (and us!): phytoplankton. These tiny plant and plant-like organisms produce more than 50% of the oxygen in our atmosphere. If we were to recover all large whale species to pre-whaling numbers, the amount of carbon sequestered would be huge and would help mitigate our rapidly changing climate.

Blue whales surfacing to breath near the Gaspe Peninsula.

Richard Sears monitoring blue whales in the Pacific population near Baja California.

BIOLOGY

Blue whales are enormous—the largest animal to have ever lived on Earth. They can grow up to 32 metres and weigh 70–132 tonnes. The Trout River blue whale is as heavy as 15 African elephants, 1.3 sauropods or 1200 adult humans. Their evolutionary adaptations to a marine environment has facilitated the great size of blue whales, and their great size profoundly influences every aspect of their life.

Aerial view of a blue whale just under the surface of the water.

Blue whale surface-feeding roll showing the expanded throat pleats.

EATING

The blue whale is the largest of all animals yet it lives off some of the smallest organisms: euphausiids (Yoo-FA-zee-ids) or krill. Small and nearly transparent, these shrimp-like animals occur in huge swarms sometimes several kilometres wide and often containing thousands of tonnes of krill. A blue whale, on average, will consume 4 tonnes of krill a day—that's about 4 million krill and 2–3 million calories. It won't always find krill, however, and will sometimes go days or weeks without a meal. Because krill are the only thing blue whales eat, they are extreme specialists. This means there is a very tight ecological relationship between krill and blue whales.

Blue whales belong to the mysticete group of whales. Instead of teeth, these whales have baleen—hard plates made of keratin, the same substance that forms hooves, claws, and human fingernails. Baleen grows in overlapping plates along the upper jaw. The plates hang down like open vertical blinds that have been pushed together. Their inner edges, the ones that face into the whale's mouth, end as long filaments—a mesh of bristles—that filter krill from the water.

Blue whales lunge feed: they open their huge mouths while lunging through the water, taking in a large gulp of krill. Blue whales, like other rorqual species, have special accordion-like pleats under their chin and chest that enlarge to form a pouch as their jaw opens and takes in water. They also have

Blue whale surface feeding in the Gulf of St. Lawrence.

a tongue that can invert backward (imagine a sock being pushed inside out) to maximize the gulp. After gulping, muscles work to expel the water through the baleen, but the krill get caught.

Lunge feeding is the largest biological action in the world. The immense drag created when the whale opens its mouth stops the blue whale completely, despite its swimming speed and massive size. During a lunge, the jaws open to 90 degrees as they rotate outwards. How does a blue whale eat without hurting itself? A special ligament, called the frontomandibular stay, helps secure the jaw. The jaw joint itself is tough and fibrous. Even the nerves supplying the mouth and tongue are specialized: they can stretch, like bungee cords, to twice their length without tearing.

In the Gulf of St. Lawrence, krill live in relatively shallow water from depths of 60 to 200 metres, so blue whales often feed close to the surface. This can be dangerous: whales can be hit by ships, and ice packs can quickly form and restrict their ability to surface. The nine whales that died in 2014 were trapped by ice, and the one that landed in Rocky Harbour was full of digested krill.

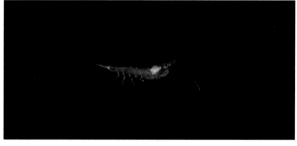

Top: A swarm of krill.

Bottom: Krill measure around 2.5 cm. This krill is shown at actual size of 2.5 cm.

BREATHING AND DIVING

How does an animal that spends a lot of time diving in the ocean for food breathe? One adaptation that has evolved in whales is the blowhole, the entrance into the whale's nasal passages. It is on top of the head instead of on the front of the snout, allowing the whale to breathe without rising too far out of the water.

The blue whale's blowholes do not stay open all the time like our noses do. Tough, fibrous structures in the blowholes function like plugs to keep them closed. Powerful muscles must act on these "plugs" to open the blowholes, and the action produces a V-shaped "splash guard" that prevents sea water from getting in when the whale surfaces to breathe.

Respiration in cetaceans is extremely efficient. When breathing normally, humans exchange about 10–15 percent of the air in our lungs. Cetaceans exchange as much as 80–90 percent. For the blue whale, this means more carbon dioxide is removed and more oxygen is loaded with each breath. Cetaceans also have more oxygen in their muscles than in their blood, creating a reservoir when they dive.

Whales breathe out by rapidly expelling vast quantities of lung air through their blowholes. Whale "blow" is an intense action. The warm air from the lungs becomes vaporized and includes droplets of oil from the respiratory tract. The shape and size of a blow is unique to each whale species, allowing us to identify individual species.

Blue whales can dive down to about 500 meters but usually stay closer to the surface, because this is where most of the krill they eat are found. Foraging dives during the day are deeper than those at night to match the movements of krill, which spend their days at greater depths. A foraging dive typically lasts 4–8 minutes, though dives of up to 20 minutes occur rather frequently.

Blue whales do not typically raise their fluke out of the water before diving. It is more common in populations from Baja California, and very rare in the Northwest Atlantic.

IDENTIFYING WHALE BLOW

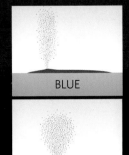

BLUE

HUMPBACK

RIGHT

SPERM

Blue whale blow, or expelled lung air, can reach a staggering height of 10 to 12 meters.

THE BRAIN

The super-sized blue whale has one of the biggest brains in the animal kingdom. It weighs 6 to 7 kg. By comparison, the human brain weighs about 1.4 kg. The biggest brain in the animal kingdom belongs to the sperm whale and weighs nearly 8 kg.

How intelligent are whales? We don't know for sure, but we can speculate by comparing their brains to those of other animals. In humans, for example, attention, judgment and social awareness are related to intellectual activity. Specific regions and structures of the human brain that relate to these cognitive functions are also highly developed in the whale brain—sometimes even more so! As in human brains, the surface of the cetacean "higher" brain (the neocortex) is wrinkled, or folded, and it is generally accepted that this development is correlated to intelligence. Many whales, including rorquals, also have special nerve cells in the brain called von Economo neurons. These cells are also present in other species that are considered to be intelligent: elephants, great apes, and humans. Finally, regions of the brain that are important for processing sound are especially well-developed in whales.

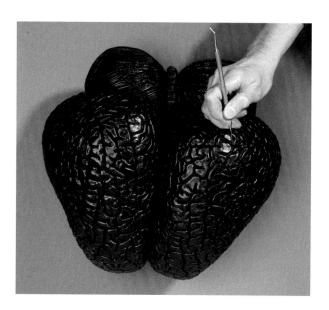

A model of the blue whale brain in the making. This model will be used to create a cast for exhibition.

FAST FACT A big body doesn't automatically come with a big brain. Giant sauropod dinosaurs were huge but had walnut-sized brains.

BRAIN SIZE COMPARISON

SAUROPOD
ENDOCAST

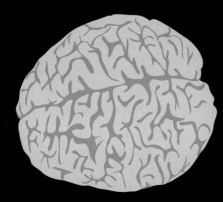

HUMAN BRAIN

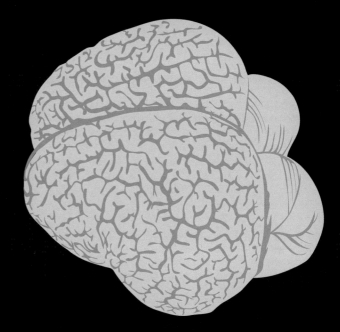

WHALE BRAIN

THE HEART

The tremendous volume of blood needed to supply the massive blue whale is circulated by an immense heart. The heart shares the basic anatomy of other mammalian hearts, including our own, but has several important differences. For example, the heart of a blue whale is wider than it is long. It is also more symmetrical in shape instead of conical like the heart of a typical land mammal, including humans.

Size is relative. In most land mammals, the heart is about 0.5–1.0 percent of total body weight. By comparison, the heart of a large whale like a blue is only 0.3–0.5 percent of its weight. A blue whale's heart is big, but not as big compared to its body size as the hearts of other mammals. As for blood, the ratio of blood volume to body weight in whales is similar to that of the hoofed mammals that are whales' closest living relatives.

The ROM's blue whale heart is the first preserved specimen of its kind and already we have learned a lot about its anatomy and physiology. For example, it is not as large as expected considering the overall size of the blue whale, and the great vessels are not as wide as we anticipated. A blue whale's heart also has two apices instead of a single apex like most land mammals, including humans.

The partially plastinated Rocky Harbour blue whale heart flanked by Jacqueline Miller and Mark Engstrom who were inspecting the preservation process at Gubener Plastinate in Germany.

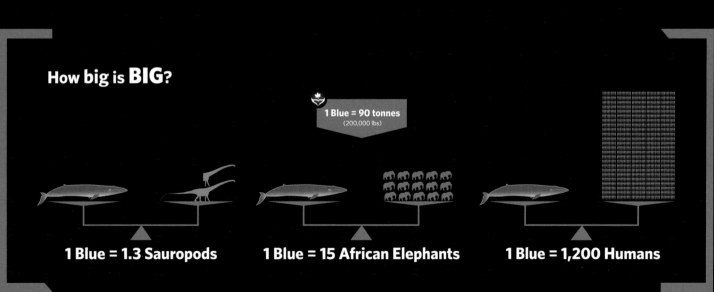

How big is **BIG**?

1 Blue = 90 tonnes
(200,000 lbs)

1 Blue = 1.3 Sauropods

1 Blue = 15 African Elephants

1 Blue = 1,200 Humans

MATING AND RAISING YOUNG

Blue whales generally travel alone, but they can sometimes be found in pairs, including mother and young. Small groups of whales can also congregate if food is abundant. Females are somewhat larger than males, and when travelling in a pair the female is usually in the lead. Sometimes three whales are seen together, as a second male tries to intervene between a male-female pair. The competition that ensues can lead to vigorous chases and rare, spectacular breaches. This behaviour is called coursing and intense fighting, called a rumba, often erupts between the males. The speed and strength of this otherwise "gentle giant" suddenly becomes apparent.

  Blue whales are thought to live 70–90 years, but their actual life span is not known. They can breed several times during their adult life. They give birth about once every three years and generally have only one baby, or calf, at a time. In the northern hemisphere, calves are typically born in November through December.

Mother and
calf surfacing.

Two blue whales in the Gulf of St. Lawrence. Blue whales do not breach dramatically like humpbacks, but on rare occasions are observed coursing (males racing to intercept females).

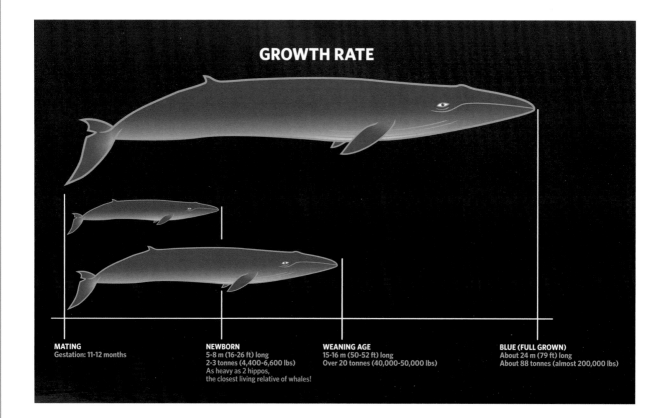

GROWTH RATE

MATING
Gestation: 11-12 months

NEWBORN
5-8 m (16-26 ft) long
2-3 tonnes (4,400-6,600 lbs)
As heavy as 2 hippos,
the closest living relative of whales!

WEANING AGE
15-16 m (50-52 ft) long
Over 20 tonnes (40,000-50,000 lbs)

BLUE (FULL GROWN)
About 24 m (79 ft) long
About 88 tonnes (almost 200,000 lbs)

Raising a baby blue whale is no small feat. A baby blue whale spends 11–12 months in its mother's womb. At birth, the baby is 7–8 metres long and weighs nearly 3 tonnes. It will grow at an average rate of 90 kilograms per day for about 7 months—equal to approximately 4 kilograms per hour! To maintain this astonishing rate of growth, a baby drinks as much as 225 litres (about 50 gallons) of milk a day.

Blue whale milk is rich—it is nearly half fat and has the consistency of heavy cream—but drinking it is a challenge for calves because they cannot suckle. Instead, they use the tip of their tongue to stimulate a blast of milk from mom, which they channel back into their throat with their tongue.

For all their great size, we still know little about when, where, or how often blue whales of the North Atlantic breed, or where they go to calve their young.

Current research conducted by the Department of Fisheries and Oceans and the Mingan Island Cetacean Study has shown that 20 satellite tagged blue whales have travelled from the Gulf of St. Lawrence in late fall, out into the Atlantic continental shelves, and then south along the eastern shore of the United States. By January and February, some animals have been documented along the mid-Atlantic ridge. There is a hypothesis that blues are using this area to breed.

NUTRITION FACTS: MAMMAL MILK COMPARISONS

Blue whales have richer milk to help the babies grow so fast. Compare how whale milk stacks up against cow milk and human milk.

	Protein %	Water %	Mineral/carb %	Fat %
Cow	3	88	5	4
Human	1	88	7	4
Blue whale	13	33	14	40

COMMUNICATING

Blue whales produce different calls that are linked to form a sequence, and that sequence is repeated many times to form a "song." Each call and each sequence is consistent and repeatable. The genetically distinct populations of blue whales are each characterized by differences in the calls and sequences of their songs—they have "dialects."

Blue whale calls are very low in frequency and most of their sound energy is "infrasonic," meaning below the threshold of human hearing. Frequencies this low can travel over very long distances undistorted, and the sounds blue whales make have been known to carry over hundreds of kilometres. These and other characteristics of blue whale calls may help them locate other whales over a large expanse of ocean or their calls may have some function in helping to locate large underwater features.

Sound travels faster in water than in air so blue whale songs cover longer distances in less time than would the same sound made in air.

SPEED OF SOUND IN AIR - 343 M/S
SPEED OF SOUND IN WATER - 1,484 M/S

Low frequency sounds have longer wavelengths and high frequency sounds (such as the calls of bats) the have shorter wavelengths. Long wavelengths carry greater distances being less prone to scatter, distortion and attenuation than short wavelengths, and the low, deep call of the blue whale travels much further (more than 1,000 kilometres) while the high pitched, ultrasonic call of a bat travels only a few tens of metres, at best.

HOW LOUD IS A BLUE WHALE?

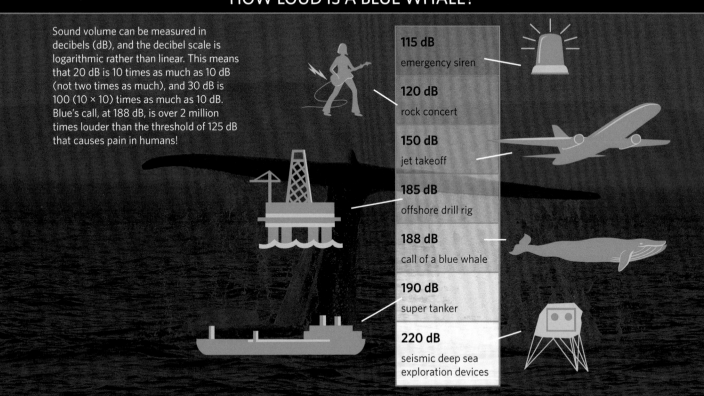

Sound volume can be measured in decibels (dB), and the decibel scale is logarithmic rather than linear. This means that 20 dB is 10 times as much as 10 dB (not two times as much), and 30 dB is 100 (10 × 10) times as much as 10 dB. Blue's call, at 188 dB, is over 2 million times louder than the threshold of 125 dB that causes pain in humans!

115 dB
emergency siren

120 dB
rock concert

150 dB
jet takeoff

185 dB
offshore drill rig

188 dB
call of a blue whale

190 dB
super tanker

220 dB
seismic deep sea exploration devices

NOISE POLLUTION

Giant whales have been living in relatively quiet waters for most of their evolution. But today, new low-frequency sounds are polluting the waters—drilling, explosions, low frequency sonar, and the sounds generated by large ships. These sounds make the oceans very noisy places and can mask or interfere with whale songs. There is growing evidence that marine noise is reducing the effective distance over which blue whales can communicate, and may also be interfering with their emission of certain types of calls. Would the ROM's blue whale have been able to find a partner in her new noisy world, especially with numbers so low?

A whale swims in a commercial sea channel near oil rigs.

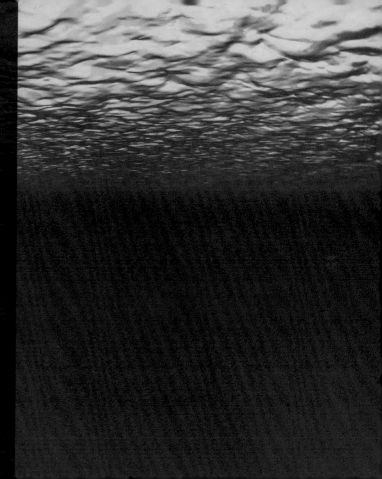

THE SOFAR SEA CHANNEL

Sound in water is affected by temperature and pressure, which cause sound to "bend" towards the colder deeper layers, then bend back up again when it encounters increasing pressure. This is referred to as the SOFAR channel (SOund Fixing And Ranging), and is an important pathway in blue whale communication. This channel is preferred for long distance communication because sound travels further in it.

EVOLUTION

Despite superficial similarities to fish, whales are not fish—they are air-breathing mammals whose ancestors lived exclusively on land! Only in the last 30 years have early whale fossils come to light and enabled scientists to reconstruct their evolutionary history—and the answers are surprising.

WHAT IS A WHALE?

Whales are aquatic vertebrates—they live in water and have a backbone. They have a streamlined body to move through water efficiently and fins, such as the tail flukes, which help stabilize the body as it swims forward.

   The Greek philosopher Aristotle described whales as having affinities to other mammals, but he kept them separate because of their fully aquatic habits. The 18th-century Swedish naturalist Linnaeus was the first to define mammals as warm-blooded, four-legged animals that give birth to live young and to include whales within them. Scientists have since verified these observations and grouped whales with dolphins and porpoises under the scientific name Cetacea. Some telltale mammalian features of whales are mammary (milk-producing) glands and hair, although these hairs are few, short, and noticeable only around the mouth and face of some species. Less obvious features that point to whales

An evolutionary tree of mammals presented by the esteemed German zoologist Ernst Haeckel in 1866. He depicted whales as closely related to artiodactyls and even more closely related to hippos—both of which scientists today regard as correct.

being mammals, include sharing fundamentally the same internal anatomical detail as other mammals and highly similar DNA.

WHALES' CLOSEST RELATIVES

Today, scientists agree that whales belong to a group of hoofed, mainly plant-eating mammals called *artiodactyls*. This group includes cows, sheep, goats, deer, pigs, hippos, and camels. Artiodactyls are one of two groups of living mammals with hooves. Artiodactyls tend to have an even number of toes (two or four), while the other group, the perissodactyls (horses, rhinos, and tapirs) tend to have one or three toes. Recent whales, of course, have highly modified limbs and have lost their toes (and hooves) entirely. But they used to have them.

  Evidence suggesting that whales are artiodactyls was presented as far back as the late 1700s. The first hints were similarities in the anatomy of their digestive and reproductive systems. During the 1950s, studies of proteins in blood also suggested a close relationship between whales and artiodactyls, as have more recent analyses of DNA. Several DNA studies even point to the hippopotamus as the closest living relative of whales. These data all suggest that whales and other artiodactyls share a common ancestor.

  Palaeontologists had only bones and teeth to study (soft

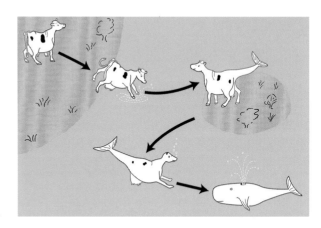

This creationist caricature (1984) of the evolution of whales was snarkily called the "Bossie to Blowhole" hypothesis.

FOSSIL WHALES PROVIDE IMPORTANT CLUES

Although the whale–artiodactyl relationship is now firmly established, scientists only reached agreement on this link about 30 years ago. Before then, many palaeontologists weren't convinced. This isn't surprising—in many ways whales appear radically different from other mammals, and direct comparisons are difficult. For example, the bones in the ankle can provide important clues about relationships between mammals. It's fairly easy to compare foot bones among cats, dogs, and seals, but in modern whales the hind leg has virtually disappeared. We see similar radical differences between whales and other animals in other aspects of their anatomy.

For a long time, all the fossil whales available were very similar to modern whales. This told palaeontologists little about earlier whales and the evolutionary origin of the group. Palaeontologists had only bones and teeth to study (soft tissue structures almost never fossilize), and dental evidence suggested that whales were most closely related to certain archaic meat-eating mammals (*mesonychids*).

Then, in the 1980s, paleontologists began discovering fossils that appeared to belong to ancient whales—much older than any they had seen before, and complete with hind limbs and ankles! Now they could compare those to other mammals, both whales and terrestrial (land-based) mammals. Critical clues came from an ear bone and an anklebone. When scientists found a whale-like ear and an artiodactyl-like

TELLTALE BONES IN *PAKICETUS*

The *astragalus* is an anklebone. In mammals, the astragalus typically has a pulley-shaped upper end and a flattened lower end. In artiodactyls and early whales that still have a foot, both ends are pulley-shaped.

The *ectotympanic* is an ear bone. In whales, this bone has two unique features: a thickened edge (the involucrum) and a small projection (the sigmoid process).

These casts of the original specimens are courtesy of Hans Thewissen.

ankle in the same fossil skeleton of a terrestrial mammal, they became convinced that whales are artiodactyls—that they came from the same ancestor. That fossil skeleton is of *Pakicetus*, which scientists consider the first whale.

WHALES AND MACROEVOLUTION

Significant steps resulting in major evolutionary change, or macroevolution, are often fleeting and difficult to discover in the fossil record and the absence of evidence is sometimes used as ammunition to criticize evolution. Because of lack of fossil evidence, naturalist Charles Darwin working in the mid to late-19th century, was vexed by whale evolution. In an early edition of his landmark book, *On the Origin of Species*, he mused about how a mammal such as a bear could through natural selection have become more adapted for marine life and could possibly result in a new species "as monstrous as a whale," (Darwin, 1859: 184). It was a thought experiment, not a description of a known event, but it drew such heavy criticism that he avoided any discussion that explicitly linked bears and whales in future editions of his book. Later, when geneticists in 1984 suggested that whales are related to artiodactyls, creationists ridiculed the idea. Unlike Darwin, however, the geneticists had more evidence, and there was much more to come.

Successive discoveries of more ancient fossil whales followed soon after, revealing many of the intermediate steps in

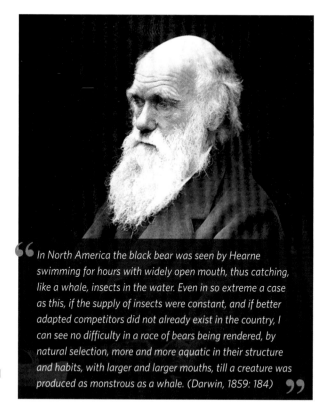

" *In North America the black bear was seen by Hearne swimming for hours with widely open mouth, thus catching, like a whale, insects in the water. Even in so extreme a case as this, if the supply of insects were constant, and if better adapted competitors did not already exist in the country, I can see no difficulty in a race of bears being rendered, by natural selection, more and more aquatic in their structure and habits, with larger and larger mouths, till a creature was produced as monstrous as a whale. (Darwin, 1859: 184)* "

whale evolution and silenced the skeptics. The fossils helped scientists fill in the details of how whales went from living on land to living in water.

Why were so many fossil whales found "all of a sudden?" Because we finally knew where to begin looking—in the rocks of Indo-Pakistan—where a few serendipitous fossils were initially discovered. Many researchers became interested in fossil whales as a result, and the rate of discoveries and research increased. Indeed, fossil whales have now been discovered that look vaguely similar to everything from large-headed dogs, to crocodiles and otters, in addition to more conventional looking whales. Today, the whale is such a well-documented example of a major evolutionary transition from land to sea that it's considered a poster child for macroevolution.

Opposite: Charles Darwin (1809–1882). The great British naturalist and geologist is primarily noted for his theory of evolution and natural selection. Beginning with his voyage of exploration on the HMS Beagle in the early 1830s, Darwin first presented a comprehensive treatment of these subjects in *On the Origin of Species* (1859). The fundamental components of his ideas—still considered as correct—are that natural selection acts on variation within a species to produce descent with modification (evolutionary change over time).

In 2001, two scientific papers on early whales appeared in major publications one day apart, on September 20 (*Nature*) and September 21 (*Science*).

HOW WHALES EVOLVED

The fossils of numerous early species have revealed when and how whales evolved from fully terrestrial to fully aquatic mammals. Among the many changes are those related to locomotion and hearing.

PAKICETIDS   These wolf-like, carnivorous, earliest whales were fully terrestrial but adept in water. They lived near coasts and waded in rivers. Some of their bones were very dense and acted as ballast while walking on river beds. They swam by paddling with all four limbs, the same as most terrestrial mammals. Their ears were like those of air-hearing mammals, but the ectotympanic had an involucrum, which helps in underwater hearing.

AMBULOCETIDS   These amphibious whales walked on land but were more adept in water than pakicetids. They lived near river mouths and swam by paddling or swinging their enormous hind feet up and down. With eyes on top of the head and nostrils near the tip of the snout, they were ambush predators, much like alligators. Their ears could hear both in air and underwater because of a unique contact between the lower jawbone and ear region.

REMINGTONOCETIDS   These amphibious whales were probably more marine-adapted than ambulocetids. They lived in marshy and swampy near-shore environments and used their sharp and pointy front teeth to prey on fish.

Pakicetids

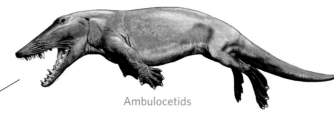

Ambulocetids

Kutchicetus

Their short thighs, not particularly well suited for terrestrial locomotion, were likely more useful for swimming, as was a flattened tail. Their ears were better able to hear underwater, an ability facilitated by ear bones that were less firmly attached to other skull bones.

PROTOCETIDS This large group includes forms such as *Maiacetus*, which was primarily aquatic but still tied to the land. Their hip bones were firmly attached to their spinal column, although their limbs were relatively short. They likely returned to land to give birth, similar to modern seals. In more advanced protocetids, such as *Georgiacetus*, the hind limbs are not attached to the spinal column and thus unable to support their bodies on land. Such whales must have been the first fully aquatic whales.

BASILOSAURIDS These fossil whales were fully aquatic with flattened, flipper-like forelimbs and relatively immobile wrists. Their hind limbs were tiny, but projected, fin-like, beyond the body outline. Basilosaurids were therefore unable to support themselves on land; they ate, reproduced, and gave birth in water. They used their tail fluke to swim like modern whales. Their sense of hearing was excellent, and the isolation of the ectotympanic bone from other skull bones allowed basilosaurids to track the source of sound waves. As in modern toothed whales, sound waves were received by the lower jaw and transferred to the ear region by a fatty pad located between the jaw and ear.

Maiacetus

Dorudon

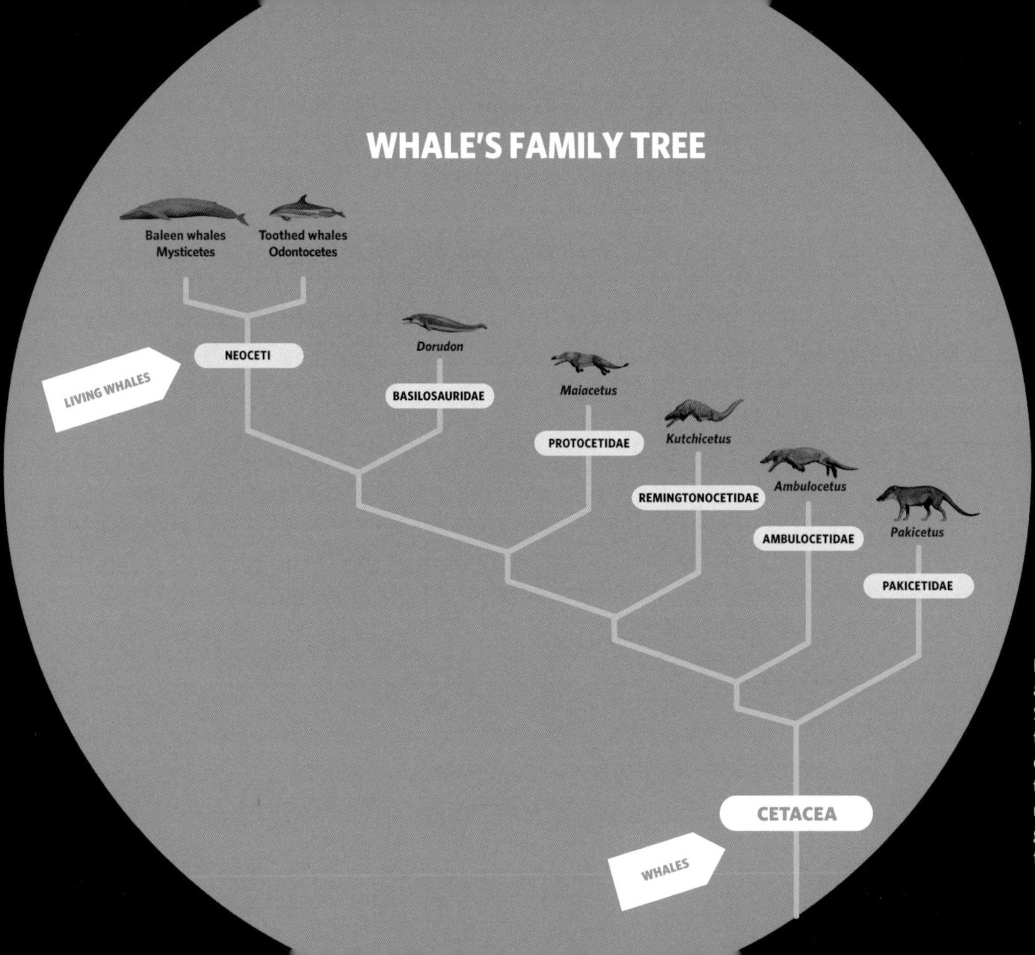

WHALE'S FAMILY TREE

Baleen whales
Mysticetes

Toothed whales
Odontocetes

Dorudon

Maiacetus

Kutchicetus

Ambulocetus

Pakicetus

NEOCETI

BASILOSAURIDAE

PROTOCETIDAE

REMINGTONOCETIDAE

AMBULOCETIDAE

PAKICETIDAE

LIVING WHALES

CETACEA

WHALES

Evolution of Living and Fossil Whales. Similar to a family tree, this branching diagram outlines the evolutionary relationships among groups of living and fossil whales.

MODERN WHALES

Living whales are included in Neoceti, a group that originated about 34 million years ago and are represented today by nearly 90 species. There are two groups of living neocetes, the odontocetes (toothed whales) and mysticetes (baleen whales). The toothed whales, with about 73 species, are more numerous, and include dolphins, porpoises, sperm and beaked whales, narwhal and beluga. They are generally smaller, although the sperm whale can reach about 20 m in length. The mysticetes are less diverse, but include the largest of the whales, including the blue whale. Other mysticetes include the fin, humpback, sei, Bryde's, minke, right, bowhead, and gray whales. Although they evolved from toothed ancestors, baleen whales lost their teeth during evolution and developed baleen plates that act as sieves to filter small prey from the water. Among mysticetes are the rorquals, species (for example, blue and fin whales) that have longitudinal pleats under the mouth and throat that allow the mouth to expand greatly during feeding. Some mysticetes, such as the gray and bowhead whales, are not rorquals. Mysticetes have two blowholes, whereas odontocetes have one. Odontocetes are also specialized in their development of echolocation: they can locate objects by emitting high frequency sounds that bounce back to the whale's ears. This ability does not seem to be present in mysticetes.

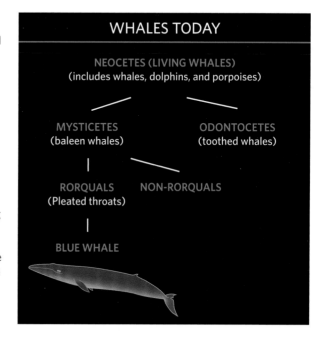

WHALES TODAY

NEOCETES (LIVING WHALES)
(includes whales, dolphins, and porpoises)

MYSTICETES
(baleen whales)

ODONTOCETES
(toothed whales)

RORQUALS
(Pleated throats)

NON-RORQUALS

BLUE WHALE

GENETICS

Whales have undergone a dramatic transformation as they have adapted from being land animals to fully aquatic creatures. The transformation can be seen both in physical changes and in the whale's DNA. At the ROM and in science labs around the world, we and our colleagues are in the process of decoding the genomes and discovering how genes have evolved to make whales masters of the seas.

WHAT IS DNA?

DNA (DeoxyriboNucleic Acid) is found in all organisms, except some viruses. It is a long, twisted molecule made of two strands that are wrapped around each other to form a double helix. The strands are held together by nucleotide bases, of which there are four: adenine, guanine, cytosine and thymidine (A,G,C,T). DNA looks like a twisted ladder, and the bases are its rungs. Since the 1940s, we have known that DNA carries the hereditary information that is passed down from parents to their offspring—a chain that stretches back, remarkably, to the origin of life. In many ways, DNA can be compared to computer code: Whereas the instructions that tell a computer what to do are written using series of 0s and 1s, the hereditary information in DNA is stored in the sequence of the four bases. DNA is the "software" of living cells.

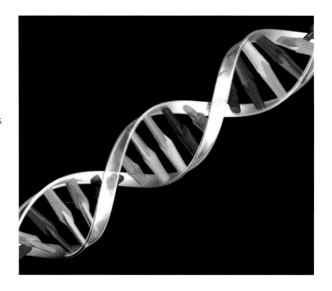

Top: Graphical representation of DNA showing how the two strands form a double helix (spiral). The backbone of each strand (white) is composed of sugar-phosphates and the two strands are held together by interactions between the nucleotide bases (coloured rods).

Opposite: DNA sequences from the two recovered blue whales for a gene only inherited from the mother. Since the two sequences are not identical (arrows show differences), they were not sisters, at least not maternally. The coloured peaks below the sequences are the raw output from the automated DNA sequencer.

WHAT IS A GENOME?

A genome is an organism's complete collection of DNA. It stores all the information necessary to build the organism and carry out the functions of its life. The genome of a blue whale contains about three billion pairs of bases, just slightly less than the number found in the human genome. The DNA itself is coiled tightly around proteins and packaged into structures known as chromosomes. There are 44 in a blue whale, 46 in a human, and 78 in a dog, even though its genome is smaller in size than both a blue whale's and a human's! During the reproductive process, each parent contributes one set of chromosomes to their offspring. The inheritance of DNA with its variation from each parent explains why offspring look like their parents and accounts

for traits being passed down through generations. It is the variation that accumulates through mutations that lead to new traits arising and this is the raw material for evolution by natural selection. Over time some of those traits which are advantageous become more widespread, while others disappear. Charles Darwin was the first to propose the theory of evolution by natural selection, but he never knew about DNA.

WHAT DOES THE WHALE'S GENOME TELL US?
MODIFIED GENES
Is it possible to know what whales see or how long some of their ancestors could hold their breath? DNA can provide insights. Whale vision has changed as these leviathans have

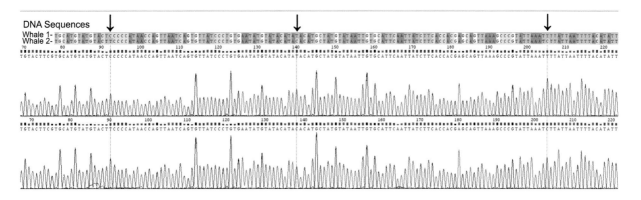

adapted to life in the ocean. By studying their genes, we know that blue whales have lost their colour vision. Their eyes now have more rods but no cones, and the cones are the cells that detect colour. The rods, however, are more sensitive to dim light. Whales have thus adapted for vision that is best suited for the dimly lit world of the ocean depths. It is no coincidence that their vision has also become more sensitive to the blue spectrum, as blue is the most abundant colour of light in deeper water although they see it as shades of gray.

Many aquatic mammals can hold their breath for exceptionally long periods of time. This allows them to fully explore and exploit their marine environment. Myoglobin is the primary oxygen-carrying molecule in muscle tissues. In whales, myoglobin exists in higher concentrations, which allows for extended dive capacity. By looking at the genes that code for myoglobin, we can see how it has been modified in whales, and by comparing it to the myoglobin in their closest living terrestrial relatives, it is possible to estimate how long some ancestral whales were able to dive and hold their breath. These times are shorter than those of modern whales, but longer than those of their land-dwelling relatives.

LOST GENES
Adult blue whales, like other mysticete whales, lack teeth and are unique among mammals in having baleen. Baleen is made of strong, flexible plates of keratin and is used to filter food directly

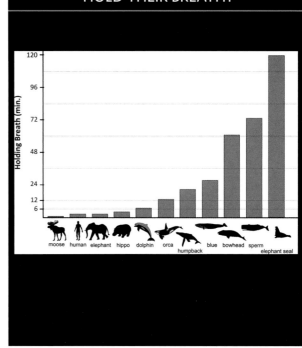

HOW LONG CAN MAMMALS HOLD THEIR BREATH?

Baleen of the Rocky Harbour blue whale being preserved for the exhibition.

from the water. Baleen whales evolved from ancestors that had teeth, and they still carry the genetic evidence of this trait. Some fossil whales between 24–28 million years old appear to have had both teeth and baleen. At some point in the evolutionary history of baleen whales, a mutation occurred that prevented the teeth from developing beyond the embryonic stage. Examination of DNA and the genes involved in making teeth reveals how these genes were inactivated in baleen whales.

POPULATION HISTORY

There is no precise historical record of how many blue whales existed in the world before commercial whaling of this species began in the late nineteenth century. One estimate places the pre-whaling worldwide population at approximately 300,000 animals. However, this number is a rough guess. Understanding how many blue whales existed before the start of whaling is crucial in knowing whether populations have recovered to their pre-whaling numbers.

The genome contains information about population history. Sequencing a blue whale's genome allows us to measure the amount of genetic diversity—the variation in the DNA between the copy inherited from the mother and the copy inherited from the father. This can shed light on the size of the ancestral population that gave rise to present-day blues and how that population changed over time. This is one of the critical questions scientists at the ROM are trying to answer using the genome we are sequencing from Blue.

Blue whale mother with her young near the Baja Peninsula.

THE NORTHWEST ATLANTIC SUBPOPULATION

Many whale species have genetically distinct populations occupying specific parts of the world's oceans, despite the waters being interconnected, and DNA analysis has helped scientists determine the boundaries of each population. Photo identification and satellite tagging are also used to help understand the structure of current populations.

We have recently discovered that culture plays a role in dividing populations in some species, where song dialects are specific to certain groups—like sperm whales in the Caribbean or humpbacks in the Northwest Pacific. Interestingly, blue whales in the North Atlantic—from the Azores to Iceland, Greenland, and the Gulf of St. Lawrence—may be one large population. One animal was observed in the Gulf in 1985, and then in the Azores in 2014, and back in the Gulf in 2015—so transatlantic movement is possible! The ROM is partnering with researchers based in the Netherlands, Scotland, and Quebec to analyze the DNA from our two blue whales to understand where they fit within the broader North Atlantic blues. What we learn will help determine if the population in the western Atlantic, where Blue was from, is part of a larger group that includes the eastern Atlantic. If this is one big genetic population, the prospects for conserving Atlantic blue whales and returning their numbers to healthier levels will be much brighter.

Blue whale surfacing near Newfoundland with the blowholes and splash guard visible. The mottling on the skin helps in photo identification of the individual whale.

THE TREE OF LIFE

Whales evolved from terrestrial mammals over millions of years and their history can be read in their DNA. The answer to where they fit in the tree of life is surprising. Comparison of DNA revealed that whales are most closely related to even-toed hoofed mammals (artiodactyls) such as hippos, pigs, deer, camels and cows—a fact later reinforced by fossils. Many questions remain to be answered about whale evolution. How are baleen whales related to each other and when did they evolve? The genome continues to be instrumental in finding the answers to questions about the ancestry and evolutionary relationships of whales.

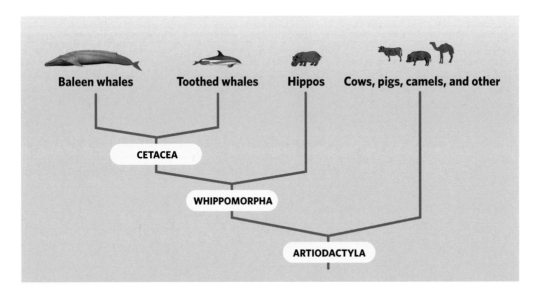

DNA data have helped resolve the relationships between whales and other mammals. The closest living relative of the whale is the hippopotamus.

MICS biologists and ROM storytellers use drone photography to help monitor a blue whale off the coast of Gaspé, Quebec in September 2016.

CONSERVATION

Protecting our oceans is fundamentally important to human sustainability: more than 70% of the surface of our Earth is covered by water, and all life and all biological processes, on land and in water, are interconnected. Conserving habitat for the great whales, including the mighty blue whale, will be a huge step toward safeguarding the ecosystems that sustain life on earth.

HUNTING BLUES

Whales have been hunted for thousands of years. Various cultures, including Indigenous communities, used the animals' meat and blubber as food, oil for fuel, and baleen for shelter and other products. When the Industrial Revolution increased demand for whale oil, whaling suddenly became a massive and very profitable business.

The blue whale's enormous bulk, speed, and typical location a long distance from shore made it a difficult target for early whalers. But with new technologies, humans managed to catch and kill about 360,000 blues for commercial whaling in the 1900s. By the mid-1960s the global blue whale population had been reduced by a staggering 98 percent.

Early harpoons were no match for blue whales, but humans were persistent. A new and improved harpoon was invented, mounted on ships, and shot from guns or cannons with intense force. It changed the whaling industry but still wasn't enough to conquer the elusive blue giants.

Illustration showing a family relaxing by lamplight in the Kawarthas. Whale oil was used in lamps before electricity.

Steam engines drove ships faster and farther in their chase for blue whales. And a big advancement was another new harpoon—one that exploded once it struck deep inside the whale. Together with new explosive harpoons, inflating blues with compressed air to keep them from sinking (other whales typically don't), and a new motorized winch to haul them on board ships opened the door to a massive slaughter of blue whales.

By the time humans managed to efficiently capture and kill blue whales, whale meat and oil were in far lower demand. Plastic had replaced baleen in most products, and petroleum meant whale oil was no longer essential. Ironically, blues, the greatest of all whales, were then hunted mainly to make soap, fertilizer, and margarine.

In 1955, the International Whaling Commission banned the hunting of blue whales in the North Atlantic. The ban was extended to the rest of the world 11 years later.

This harpoon gun from the late 1800s or early 1900s was too small to hunt blue whales. It would have been more effective against bowhead whales (Hudson's Bay Corporate Collection).

DANGEROUSLY COLD

On average, one blue whale has died every five years since the 1800s by getting trapped in sea ice in the Gulf of St. Lawrence. Why did an unprecedented nine blues die in 2014? The ice cover in the River and the Gulf has been decreasing steadily for at least the last 40 years, possibly as a result of climate change, and whales have been entering the Gulf of St. Lawrence earlier in the spring and leaving later in the fall. In an anomalously cold year like 2014, the Gulf becomes a death trap for feeding blue whales that get caught in the quickly changing and unpredictable ice build-up.

The Department of Fisheries and Oceans flew over the Gulf of St. Lawrence in late March 2014 to confirm the death of nine blue whales in the ice formations off the southwest tip of Newfoundland.

THE TOP 5 THREATS TO BLUE WHALES

The only natural predators of blue whales are killer whales and perhaps large sharks, but only calves and young animals are vulnerable. If a blue whale survives its first year, then the main threat to its survival is human activity. The following threats to blue whales are ranked in order of severity:

1 NOISE POLLUTION   Low frequency sounds from shipping, military sonar, seismic exploration, and oil and gas development interfere with social communication. Blue whales have been living in relatively quiet waters for most of their history. Finding a mate in their new noisy world, especially with numbers so low, has become increasingly difficult.

2 POLLUTED WATER   The Gulf of St. Lawrence remains heavily contaminated with PCB pollutants that come primarily from the highly industrialized Great Lakes. This contaminated water poisons blue whales. The situation is made worse by trash, chemical cleaners, plastics, and gasoline that make their way into the ocean, even from our own waters in the Toronto region.

3 SHIP STRIKES   Blues are fast and big. But ships have become faster and bigger. Collisions with cruise ships and commercial vessels are a deadly threat: some scientists suggest about 70% of these strikes are fatal.

4 HUMAN-INDUCED CLIMATE CHANGE: ICE AND FOOD
Climate change impacts all life on Earth. For blue whales, the negative consequences are changing sea ice patterns which may result in less predictable, less abundant sources of food.

5 WHALING   The only countries currently still hunting whales for commercial purposes, thereby ignoring the ban on whaling, are Norway, Iceland, and Japan. A few others continue to lobby the International Whaling Commission to let them hunt blues.

Strikes by large ships are one of the main threats to whale populations.

ECOSYSTEM ENGINEERS

Beavers, like humans, are well-known ecosystem engineers. They dam waterways by building extensive walls of mud and sticks, which creates less moving water and more wetland habitat that affects many other plants and animals.

The large baleen whales, including blues, are also ecosystem engineers. Blue whales naturally alter their habitat in two major, beneficial, ways: 1) whale falls, and 2) the whale pump. Together, these naturally mitigate climate change.

WHALE FALLS

When a 100-tonne animal dies and sinks to the ocean floor, an enormous amount of carbon, nutrients, and other essential minerals are transported to a new ecosystem in the dark depths, sometimes as much as 3 kilometres down. The entire carcass is slowly consumed, its energy and nutrients sustaining many other species for decades. Some animals only live on or near whale falls; these endemic species are threatened as fewer whale falls occur because of lower populations.

THE WHALE PUMP

One blue whale eats about 4 tonnes of krill a day. Krill eat phytoplankton (composed of tiny plants and plant-like organisms) that form the foundation of all marine food webs. These "forests of the sea" suck up about 50 percent of all human-generated carbon dioxide emissions. Phytoplankton require nutrients and sunlight, and a blue whale provides some of these nutrients in a unique way: poo. A plume of blue whale excrement is big enough to be seen from an aircraft, about 60 metres wide and 100 metres long. Whale feces have 250,000 to 10,000,000 times more vital nutrients than seawater. So, the more whales there are, the more poo there is. The more poo there is, the more phytoplankton. The more phytoplankton, the more carbon dioxide is removed from the atmosphere, and the more krill there are for blue whales to eat. Eat. Poop. Repeat.

FAST FACT

A single blue whale produces enough excrement in its lifetime to capture the same amount of carbon dioxide that 1,000 Canadians produce in a year.

Fin whales are the second largest animal on earth, and occupy similar habitats as blue whales; their fecal stream is green because they are feeding on small fish whereas a blue whale fecal stream would be orange because they feed exclusively on krill.

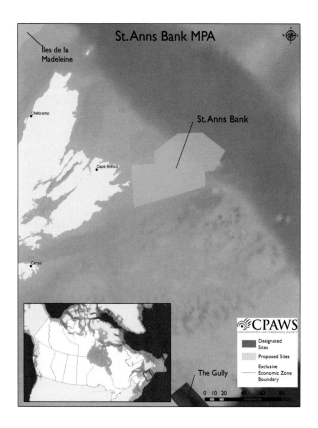

PROTECTING CANADA'S BLUE WHALES

Blue whale populations once totalled about 300,000 individuals. Today there are—at most—20,000. In the North Atlantic, numbers have dropped from over 12,000 to just 1,000. In the Northwest Atlantic there are only 200–400 individuals. Blue whales are now classified as endangered in Canadian waters and across their global range. Scientists count blue whales in the Gulf of St. Lawrence every year where they number between 30 and 110.

Canada has 202,080 kilometres of ocean coastline—more than any country in the world. Along with blue whales, countless plants, invertebrates, fishes, and marine mammals call our shores home. Some of the best feeding grounds for whales are in the Gulf of St. Lawrence. In 2016, scientists saw six species of large whales at this extraordinary site, including endangered blues and the critically endangered northern right whale.

Marine Protected Areas (MPAs) are regions of the ocean protected by law to help improve the ecosystem. As of February 2016, there were over 6,800 MPAs globally— equivalent to about 3 percent of the world's oceans. The California population of blues has rebounded to more than 90% of what it was before whaling—the only population in the world to recover, in part because of safeguarding habitat. The two largest MPAs ever created were announced in 2016 —the Papahānaumokuākea Marine National Monument in

Blue whale surfacing near the Gaspe Peninsula. The mottling on the skin and the shape of the dorsal fin are important identification features of individual whales.

Hawai'i and a large swath of the Ross Sea in Antarctica. Each represent about 1.5 million square kilometers of protected habitat—the latter is critical habitat for blue whales. MPAs are like "national parks" of the oceans.

Currently, about 1 percent of Canada's oceans are protected by MPAs. The federal government has pledged to protect 5 percent of our marine and coastal areas by 2017, and 10 percent by 2020. One of the newest Canadian MPAs is St. Anns Bank, off the shores of Cape Breton, which is approximately 4300 km^2 of protected ocean habitat close to where Blue was found. The ROM applauds the commitment of the Canadian government to protect this critical habitat and encourages the designation of a series of connected protected zones in the Gulf of St. Lawrence.

California blue whales have benefited from strong habitat protection policies.

MINGAN ISLAND CETACEAN STUDY

The world's largest and longest-running blue whale research program is located in the Gulf of St. Lawrence. It's called Mingan Island Cetacean Study (MICS) and was founded by Richard Sears in 1979.

MICS is a non-profit research group that studies all kinds of marine life and particularly the rorquals (baleen whales with pleated throats): the fin, minke, humpback, northern right, and especially blue whales. Running on a modest annual operating budget of less than $300,000, the MICS team expands to 20 or more volunteers and staff during peak season (May through September). This eclectic group of marine biologists spends time in three primary areas: Quebec's North Shore (Mingan Archipelago and Anticosti Island), the Gaspé Peninsula, and the estuary of the St. Lawrence. More recently they are collaborating with other researchers to monitor blue whales in the Azores, New Zealand, Greenland, and the Bay of Fundy.

Studying the planet's largest creatures—by nature elusive and difficult to observe—on the open ocean from small, inflatable boats is not easy. Incredible work by Richard Sears and his team from MICS has resulted in amazing new information about blue whales. The first trans-Atlantic movement of a blue whale was documented by MICS: an individual was observed in 1985 in the Gulf of St. Lawrence and in 2014 off the shores of Portugal in the Azores, and then again in the Gulf in 2015.

FAST FACT The photo identification method used by all blue whale scientists for recognizing individual animals was established by Richard Sears, and MICS compiles and curates the blue whale sightings in the North Atlantic.

MICS biologists monitor two humpback whales in the Gulf of St. Lawrence. Photography and biopsy sampling are the two primary tools used to study individuals over time.

A LEGACY OF BLUE

Here are three things you can do to support the long term protection of blue whales:

1 SUPPORT RESEARCH   Become a trail-blazing tourist and join blue whale scientists in the field. Research tourism, as pioneered by Richard Sears and MICS, makes you part of an active team studying these marine mammals. Take part in seven full days of research, including 12-hour days on the ocean. This unique form of ecotourism gives you an exceptional opportunity to observe whales from a smaller boat with experienced research biologists, who can provide in-depth information about these giants. You may have the chance to hang out with whales that have been known for several decades! Your financial contribution and the real work you do on board support the research.

Our own work at the ROM, investigating the genome of the blue whale and preparing the skeleton and heart for display, will further our collective understanding of these creatures. Join our growing lists of supporters and donors at www.rom.on.ca/en/makeasplash.

2 BECOME A CITIZEN SCIENTIST   When you see a whale, even on vacation, take a picture and send it to one of the websites listed below—remember to use your GPS or geo-tag your photos! Your photos can help scientists track whales to better understand their behaviours and identification patterns.

As citizen scientists, you will join thousands of other people who are contributing to our understanding of whales.

iNaturalist.ca ROM-led biodiversity identification program
Rorqual.com MICS photo-identification program

3 CARE FOR OUR WATER   The global water cycle is a closed loop. Every drop of freshwater eventually ends up in the oceans or the atmosphere. We all learn this in elementary school, yet our daily actions don't always support water conservation. Remember the simple things, conserve water and think of a blue whale before you flush!

Research tourist helping monitor whales on board a MICS boat.

Published by the Royal Ontario Museum with the generous support of the Louise Hawley Stone Charitable Trust. The Stone Trust generates significant annual funding for the Museum, providing a steady stream of support that is used to purchase new acquisitions and to produce publications related to the ROM's collection. The Louise Hawley Stone Charitable Trust was established in 1998 when the ROM received a charitable trust of nearly $50 million—the largest cash bequest ever received by the Museum—by its long-time friend and supporter, the late Louise Hawley Stone (1904-1997).

Royal Ontario Museum 100 Queen's Park Toronto, Ontario M5S 2C6
www.rom.on.ca

Library and Archives Canada Cataloguing in Publication
Cataloguing data available from Library and Archives Canada.

ISBN 978-0-88854-519-0

Opposite: Blue whale
breaching—a rare
behaviour for
this species.

MARK ENGSTROM is Deputy Director of Collections & Research and Senior Curator of Mammalogy at the Royal Ontario Museum.

BURTON LIM is Assistant Curator of Mammalogy at the Royal Ontario Museum.

JACQUELINE MILLER is Mammalogy Technician at the Royal Ontario Museum.

OLIVER HADDRATH is Ornithology Technician at the Royal Ontario Museum.

DAVE IRELAND is Managing Director of Biodiversity at the Royal Ontario Museum.

GERRY DE IULIIS is Lecturer in the Department of Ecology & Evolutionary Biology at the University of Toronto.

Design: Claire Louise Milne; Managing Editor: Sheeza Sarfraz; Copy Editor: Dimitra Chronopoulos; Cover Design: Rose Pereira; Editor (French): Dominique Picouet; Translation (French): Lucie Chevalier; Production Designer (French): Claire Louise Milne.

Photo credits: Fatima Ali: 57; Brian Boyle: 32, 47, 63; Don Bradshaw: 11; Carl Buell: 50, 51; Phillip Colla: 36; CPAWS: 68; EB-Quest: 29 (bottom), 54; Uko Gorter: 41; Georgia Guenther: 32 (brain model); Oliver Haddrath: 55, 56; Ernst Haeckel: 45; Tom Henriksson: 2, 10, 35, 52, 60; Richard Herrmann: 29; iStock: 8; Yoon Kang: 1; Brian Kot: 28, 31; Anne Langton: 62; Jack Lawson: 9, 64; Burton Lim: 15; Vincent Luk: 61, 65, 67, 71, 72, 73, 75; Peter May: 19; Sally McIntyre: 18; David McNew: 43; Jacqueline Miller: 20–22; Claire Louise Milne: 33, 39, 40, 42, 53, 60; Mingan Island Cetacean Study: 24, 27, 58, 59, 69, 70; 7125, 26, 30, 37; Samantha Phillips: 16; Guber Plastinate: 34; Nila Sivatheesan: 17; Luther Sunderland, in Philip Gingerich (Proceedings of the American Philosophical Society, 2012): 46; Hans Thewissen: 49 (Nature cover); Margot Thompson: 31; Asha de Vos: 66; Jacqueline Waters: 4, 12, 14; Wikipedia Commons: 6, 48.

Inside Cover Photo: Philip Colla; Back Cover Illustration: Yoon Kang

Printed and bound in Canada by Transcontinental Printing.

The Royal Ontario Museum is an agency of the Government of Ontario.